EASY THAI COOKING

Publisher: Ray Ramsay
Editor: Margaret Gore
Production Manager: Anna Maguire
Design: Karen Jeffery
Cover Design: Chrissie Lloyd
Home Economist: Pam Trotter
Cover Home Economist: Kathy Man
Food Stylist: Penny Farrell
Cover Stylist: Kay McGlone
Photography: Phil Wymant
Cover Photography: Gus Filgate

Typeset at The Typographers, North Sydney, NSW, Australia

Printed at Griffin Press Limited, Netley, South Australia

ISBN 1-875216-31-6

**Published by The Custom Book Company
15B Penrhyn Avenue, Beecroft, NSW 2119, Australia

© Custom Book Company

Distributed by J.B. Fairfax Press Ltd.
9 Trinity Centre, Park Farm Estate
Wellingborough, Northants, UK
Ph: (0933) 402330   Fax: (0933) 402234

**A joint venture of Century Magazines Pty Limited
and R.A. Ramsay Pty Limited.

WHAT'S IN A TABLESPOON?

NEW ZEALAND	1 tablespoon = 15ml OR 3 teaspoons	
UNITED KINGDOM	1 tablespoon = 15ml OR 3 teaspoons	
AUSTRALIA	1 tablespoon = 20ml OR 4 teaspoons	

The recipes in this book were tested in Australia where a 20ml tablespoon is standard. All measures are level.

The tablespoon in the New Zealand and United Kingdom sets of measuring spoons is 15ml. In many recipes this difference will not matter. For recipes using baking powder, gelatine, bicarbonate of soda, small quantities of flour and cornflour, simply add another teaspoon for each tablespoon specified.

CHILLI

CHILLI

BITTER MELON

GARLIC

DRIED MUSHROOMS

CHILLI

FRESH LEMONGRASS

CHILLI

CHILLI

WHITE RADISH

FRESH WATER CHESTNUTS

BASIL

BROWN ONION

RED ONION

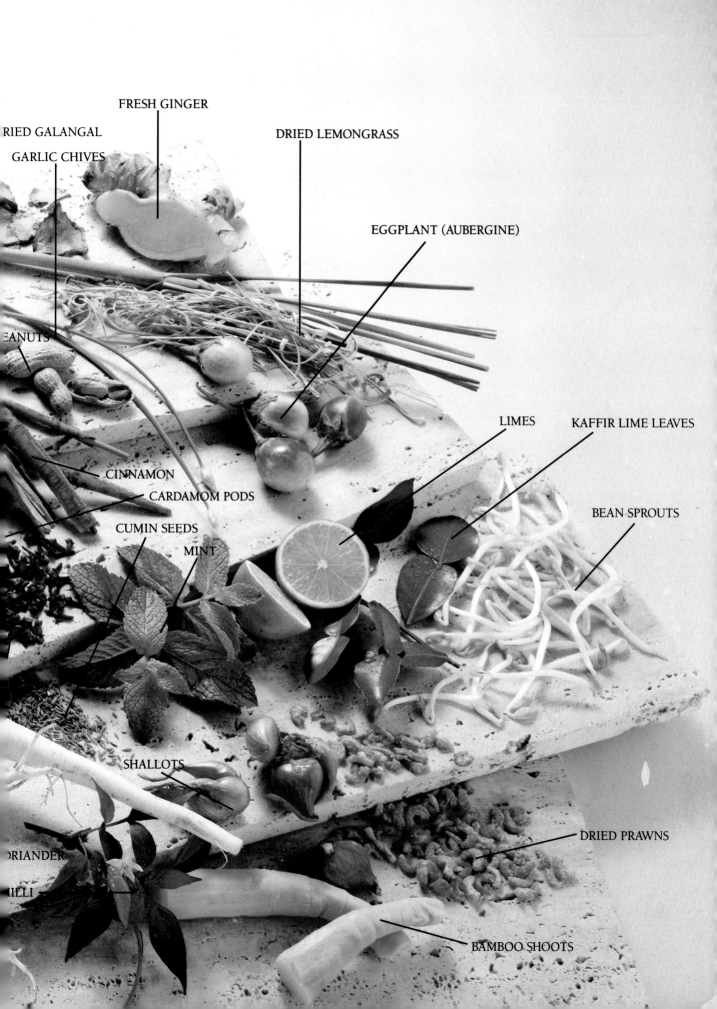

FRESH GINGER

RIED GALANGAL

GARLIC CHIVES

DRIED LEMONGRASS

EGGPLANT (AUBERGINE)

EANUTS

LIMES

KAFFIR LIME LEAVES

CINNAMON

CARDAMOM PODS

BEAN SPROUTS

CUMIN SEEDS

MINT

SHALLOTS

DRIED PRAWNS

ORIANDER

IILLI

BAMBOO SHOOTS

Thai cuisine is wonderfully varied, full of interesting textures and flavours. It combines the best aspects of a number of Oriental cuisines, including the exotic flavour of Malaysia, the tang of Szechuan Chinese, the coconut sauces of southern India and the aromatic spices of Arabia.

But, although it combines aspects of other cuisines, it has a distinctive character all its own, and it's also a healthy and nutritious style of cooking. This is because the Thais use the best of fresh ingredients: small, lean portions of meat and chicken, seafood and masses of vegetables and fruit. What gives Thai food its distinctive flavour is the use of herbs and spices such as coriander plants, fresh basil, mint and lemon grass, garlic, chillies, citrus leaves and coconut milk.

Thai food is also lightly cooked to create crisp, colourful, flavoursome dishes. The recipes in this book make Thai cuisine so simple for the home cook. They're quick and easy to prepare, and we have explained how to buy and use some of the more unusual ingredients. We're sure you and your family will enjoy these dishes, confident in the knowledge that they not only taste good but are good for you too.

CONTENTS

Appetisers

THAI SPRING ROLLS

100G/3½OZ CHICKEN FILLETS, FINELY CHOPPED

50G/2OZ PEELED RAW PRAWNS, FINELY CHOPPED

1 CARROT, GRATED

100G/3½OZ BEAN SPROUTS

2 SPRING ONIONS, SLICED

1CM/½IN CUBE PEELED FRESH GINGER, FINELY CHOPPED

2 TEASPOONS SOY SAUCE

2 TEASPOONS FISH SAUCE

2 TEASPOONS CORNFLOUR

2 TABLESPOONS WATER

1 PKT 12CM/5IN SQUARE SPRING ROLL OR WONTON WRAPPERS

1. In a bowl combine chicken, chopped prawns, carrot, bean sprouts, spring onions, ginger, soy sauce and fish sauce.
2. Mix cornflour and water together to make a thin paste. Take one spring roll wrapper at a time and place about 2 teaspoons of filling near one corner of square, fold that corner over filling and fold left and right sides into the centre. Roll up to make a cigar shape, brushing the edges of last corner with cornflour mixture before sealing.
3. Deep-fry spring rolls over a medium heat until golden brown all over. Drain on absorbent paper. Serve with Sweet Chilli Sauce. (See page 8.)
MAKES 16

BEEF AND PEANUT BUNDLES

1 TABLESPOON OIL

1 ONION, CHOPPED

1 CLOVE GARLIC, CRUSHED

250G/8OZ (½LB) MINCED BEEF

1 MEDIUM POTATO, PEELED AND FINELY CHOPPED

1 CORIANDER PLANT, INCLUDING ROOTS, CHOPPED

½ RED CHILLI, SEEDED AND FINELY CHOPPED

¼ CUP/30G/1OZ PEANUTS, CHOPPED

2 TEASPOONS SUGAR

1 TABLESPOON FISH SAUCE

1 PKT SPRING ROLL WRAPPERS

VEGETABLE OIL FOR FRYING

1. Heat oil in a saucepan and fry onion and garlic for 2 minutes. Add minced beef and fry until lightly browned.
2. Stir in potato, coriander, chilli, peanuts, sugar and fish sauce. Lower heat and cover with a lid. Cook for 15 to 20 minutes or until potato is tender.
3. Trim each spring roll wrapper into an 18cm/7in circle. Place 1 tablespoon of filling in the centre and gather up edges to make a bundle. Tie with white cotton thread.
4. Deep-fry bundles in vegetable oil until golden brown and drain on absorbent paper. Remove cotton and discard. Serve bundles with Sweet Chilli Sauce. (See page 8.)
MAKES 24

Beef and Peanut Bundles

Thai Spring Rolls

CRUNCHY PORK BALLS WITH SWEET CHILLI SAUCE

(This recipe can easily be doubled.)
250G/8OZ (½LB) MINCED BEEF
250G/8OZ (½LB) MINCED PORK
3 CLOVES GARLIC, CRUSHED
3 TABLESPOONS CHOPPED FRESH CORIANDER
½ BEATEN EGG
¼ TEASPOON NUTMEG
¼ TEASPOON BLACK PEPPER
3 TEASPOONS FISH SAUCE
1½ CUPS/280G/9OZ COOKED LONG-GRAIN RICE
VEGETABLE OIL FOR FRYING

1. Place all ingredients except rice and oil into a bowl and mix well.
2. Take heaped teaspoons of mixture and roll into balls. Coat firmly in the cooked rice.
3. Fry pork balls in about 1cm/½in of oil until they are golden brown all over. Drain on absorbent paper. Serve with Sweet Chilli Sauce. (See recipe below.)
MAKES 16

SWEET CHILLI SAUCE

(The heat of this sauce will depend on the variety of chilli used. For a milder sauce use a smaller amount of chillies and a milder variety. See Ingredient Section for information.)
12 SMALL RED CHILLIES, STEMS REMOVED
4 CLOVES GARLIC
1 CUP/250ML/8FL OZ WHITE VINEGAR
½ CUP/125G/4OZ SUGAR
1 TEASPOON SALT

1. Roughly chop chillies and garlic, place in a small saucepan with remaining ingredients. Bring to the boil, lower heat and simmer until a syrupy consistency, about 10 to 15 minutes.
2. Place in a blender or food processor and process until chillies are finely chopped. Serve warm.
Note: This sauce will keep well in the refrigerator for about 1 month if stored in a sterilised jar.
MAKES ¾ CUP/180ML/6FL OZ

SATAYS

1KG/2LB LEAN BEEF, PORK OR CHICKEN FILLETS
½ CUP/125ML/4FL OZ COCONUT MILK
1 TABLESPOON RED CURRY PASTE (SEE PAGE 72)
1 TABLESPOON FISH SAUCE
1 TEASPOON SUGAR

1. Remove fat or gristle from meat and cut into thin strips 2cm/¾in wide and about 8 to 10cm/3 to 4in long. Place in a glass or ceramic dish.
2. Mix all remaining ingredients together and pour over meat, mix well. Refrigerate for several hours or overnight. Thread the strips of meat onto satay sticks, 2 pieces per stick, by weaving the meat strips in and out along the stick. (Satay sticks can be soaked in a dish of water for several hours before using. This prevents them burning on the barbecue.)
3. Barbecue or grill satays on a high heat until brown all over. Serve hot with Peanut Sauce. (See recipe below.)
SERVES 6 TO 8 AS AN ENTRÉE

PEANUT SAUCE

1 TABLESPOON OIL
2 CLOVES GARLIC, CRUSHED
1 ONION, CHOPPED
½ RED CHILLI, SEEDED AND FINELY CHOPPED
1 STALK LEMON GRASS OR 5CM/2IN STRIP LEMON PEEL
¾ CUP/180ML/6FL OZ COCONUT MILK
1 TABLESPOON FISH SAUCE
¼ CUP/45G/1½OZ BROWN SUGAR, LIGHTLY PACKED
½ CUP/125G/4OZ CRUNCHY PEANUT BUTTER

1. Heat oil in a saucepan. Add garlic and onion and fry for 2 minutes. Stir in all remaining ingredients and bring to the boil. Lower heat and simmer for 15 minutes or until sauce has thickened.
MAKES 1 CUP/250ML/8FL OZ

Opposite: Satays and Peanut Sauce
Crunchy Pork Balls with Sweet Chilli Sauce

Thai Fish Patties

250G/8OZ (½LB) WHITE FISH FILLETS
½ CUP/90G/3OZ COOKED LONG-GRAIN RICE
½ CUP/60G/2OZ GREEN BEANS, ROUGHLY CHOPPED
1 STALK LEMON GRASS, SLICED
2 CLOVES GARLIC, CRUSHED
1 RED CHILLI, SEEDS REMOVED AND CHOPPED
1 CORIANDER PLANT, ROOTS INCLUDED, CHOPPED
2 TEASPOONS FISH SAUCE
1 EGG, BEATEN
VEGETABLE OIL FOR FRYING

1. Remove any skin and bones from fish and cut into pieces. Place into a food processor with all remaining ingredients except oil. Process until ingredients are just combined, don't overmix.
2. Shape heaped tablespoonsful of mixture into patties. Fry patties a few at a time in about 1cm/½ in of oil until golden brown on both sides. Drain on absorbent paper. Serve with Pickled Cucumber Salad. (See recipe below.)
MAKES 10

Pickled Cucumber Salad

1 SMALL TO MEDIUM CUCUMBER, PEELED
¼ CUP/60ML/2FL OZ WATER
1 TABLESPOON SUGAR
¼ CUP/60ML/2FL OZ WHITE VINEGAR
2CM/¾IN CUBE PEELED FRESH GINGER, FINELY CHOPPED
½ SMALL RED CHILLI, SEEDED AND SLICED

1. Cut cucumber in half lengthwise and remove seeds. Slice thinly and place into a bowl.
2. Heat water and sugar in a small saucepan until sugar has dissolved. Remove from heat, add vinegar and ginger and pour over cucumber, mix well. Refrigerate for 30 minutes, sprinkle with chilli before serving.
SERVES 4 TO 6

Prawn Toasts

100G/3½OZ RAW PEELED PRAWNS, FINELY CHOPPED
100G/3½OZ PORK MINCE
2 SPRING ONIONS, CHOPPED
2 CLOVES GARLIC, CRUSHED
½ CORIANDER PLANT, INCLUDING ROOTS, CHOPPED
½ BEATEN EGG
3 TEASPOONS FISH SAUCE
½ TEASPOON GROUND BLACK PEPPER
5 SLICES WHITE BREAD, CRUSTS REMOVED
VEGETABLE OIL FOR FRYING

1. Place all ingredients except bread and oil in a bowl and mix well.
2. Spread prawn mixture evenly over each slice of bread, right to the edges. Cut each slice into 4 squares.
3. Deep-fry the squares in vegetable oil, prawn-side down, until golden brown. Drain on absorbent paper. Keep each batch warm in a very low oven while you fry the remainder. Serve with Radish in Vinegar. (See recipe below.)
MAKES 20 PRAWN TOASTS

Radish In Vinegar

4 TABLESPOONS GRATED WHITE OR RED RADISH
¼ CUP/60ML/2FL OZ WHITE VINEGAR
3 TEASPOONS CASTER SUGAR
SALT

1. Mix radish, vinegar and caster sugar together. Add salt to taste. Spoon into a small dish and serve.
SERVES 4

Opposite: Thai Fish Patties, Prawn Toasts and Condiments

GALLOPING HORSES

1 TABLESPOON OIL
250G/8OZ (½LB) LEAN PORK MINCE
4 SPRING ONIONS, CHOPPED
1 CLOVE GARLIC, CRUSHED
2 TABLESPOONS BROWN SUGAR, LIGHTLY PACKED
1 CORIANDER PLANT, INCLUDING ROOTS, CHOPPED
1 TABLESPOON FISH SAUCE
¼ TEASPOON GROUND BLACK PEPPER
¼ CUP/30G/1OZ FINELY CHOPPED PEANUTS
FRESH PINEAPPLE SLICES AND FRESH ORANGES

1. Heat oil in a frying pan, add pork mince, spring onions and garlic and fry until mince has changed colour, about 4 minutes.
2. Add all remaining ingredients except peanuts and fruit and continue cooking until pork is well browned and mixture is crumbly. Remove from heat, stir in peanuts and set aside to cool.
3. Cut pineapple slices into bite-sized pieces. Peel oranges and cut into thick slices. Arrange fruit on a serving platter. Place a spoonful of meat mixture onto each piece of fruit and serve.
SERVES 4 TO 6

LEMON CALAMARI SALAD

(This salad is delicious served on a bed of lettuce or other salad greens.)
500G/1LB CLEANED CALAMARI (SQUID)
1 RED CHILLI, SEEDED AND FINELY SLICED
CHILLI LEMON DRESSING
½ CUP/125ML/4FL OZ LEMON JUICE
2 TEASPOONS CASTER SUGAR
1 TABLESPOON FISH SAUCE
2 STALKS LEMON GRASS, FINELY SLICED
4 SPRING ONIONS, SLICED
2 TABLESPOONS CHOPPED FRESH MINT

1. Slice calamari into thin rings and cook in a saucepan of boiling water for 1 to 2 minutes or until calamari is just cooked. Don't overcook or it will become tough. Drain well and place in a bowl.
2. *Chilli Lemon Dressing:* Place all dressing ingredients in a jar and shake well.
3. Pour dressing over calamari and refrigerate until well chilled. Sprinkle with sliced chilli before serving.
SERVES 4 TO 6

Opposite: Galloping Horses

Lemon Calamari Salad

Soups

CLEAR MUSHROOM AND CORN SOUP

4 CHINESE DRIED MUSHROOMS

425G/13OZ CAN BABY CORN

1 TABLESPOON OIL

2 CLOVES GARLIC, CRUSHED

½ TEASPOON GROUND BLACK PEPPER

1 CORIANDER PLANT, ROOTS INCLUDED, CHOPPED

1 ONION, CHOPPED

200G/7OZ LEAN PORK, CHOPPED

4 CUPS/1 LITRE/1¾ PINTS WATER

2 TABLESPOONS FISH SAUCE

1 TABLESPOON FRESHLY CHOPPED BASIL

1. Soak dried mushrooms in boiling water for 30 minutes. Drain and slice. Drain baby corn and rinse well, cut into bite-sized pieces.
2. Heat oil in a large saucepan, add garlic, pepper, coriander and onion and fry for 2 minutes. Add chopped pork and fry until pork is golden brown.
3. Add water, fish sauce, baby corn and mushrooms and bring to the boil. Lower heat, cover with a lid and simmer for 10 minutes. Serve hot, sprinkled with chopped basil leaves.
SERVES 4

SPICY PRAWN AND LEMON GRASS SOUP

4 CUPS/1 LITRE/1¾ PINTS WATER

4 SPRING ONIONS, SLICED

2CM/¾IN CUBE PEELED FRESH GINGER, CHOPPED

2 STALKS LEMON GRASS, THINLY SLICED

2 DRIED KAFFIR LIME LEAVES

2 CLOVES GARLIC, CHOPPED

1 RED CHILLI, SEEDED

2 TABLESPOONS FISH SAUCE

200G/7OZ RAW PEELED PRAWNS

1 TABLESPOON LEMON JUICE

1. Place all ingredients except prawns and lemon juice into a large saucepan and bring to the boil. Lower heat, cover with a lid and simmer for 15 minutes.
2. Add peeled prawns and lemon juice and cook for a further 3 minutes or until prawns are just cooked. Don't overcook or prawns will become tough. Remove whole chilli and kaffir leaves before serving.
SERVES 4

*Clear Mushroom
and Corn Soup*

*Spicy Prawn and
Lemon Grass Soup*

Coconut and Chicken Soup

4 CUPS/1 LITRE/1¾ PINTS COCONUT MILK

1 LARGE ONION, CHOPPED

1 STALK LEMON GRASS, THINLY SLICED

2CM/¾IN CUBE PEELED FRESH GINGER, CHOPPED

2 RED CHILLIES, SEEDED

250G/8OZ CHICKEN THIGH OR BREAST FILLETS

2 TABLESPOONS CHOPPED CORIANDER

---

1. Place coconut milk, onion, lemon grass, ginger and whole chillies into a medium saucepan and bring to the boil.
2. Cut chicken into small bite-sized pieces and add to saucepan. Lower heat and simmer for 15 minutes or until chicken is tender. Serve sprinkled with chopped coriander. Remove chillies before serving.
SERVES 4

Rice Soup

(In Thailand this soup is often eaten for breakfast.)

1 TABLESPOON OIL

3 CLOVES GARLIC, CHOPPED

200G/7OZ LEAN PORK, CHOPPED

6 CUPS/1.5 LITRES/2½ PINTS CHICKEN STOCK

6 SPRING ONIONS, CHOPPED

1 TABLESPOON FISH SAUCE

⅔ CUP/140G/4½OZ LONG-GRAIN RICE

1 CORIANDER PLANT, CHOPPED

---

1. Heat oil in a large saucepan, add garlic and pork and fry until pork is golden brown.
2. Stir in chicken stock, spring onions, fish sauce and rice and bring to the boil. Lower heat and simmer for 15 to 20 minutes or until soup is like thin porridge.
3. Serve soup immediately, sprinkled with chopped coriander.
SERVES 4 TO 6

Fish Curry Soup

(The shrimp paste in this recipe is optional, however it does add an extra flavour that really enhances the soup.)

250G/8OZ WHITE FISH FILLETS

1 TABLESPOON OIL

1 TABLESPOON GREEN CURRY PASTE (SEE PAGE 72)

½ TEASPOON TURMERIC

½ CUP/100G/3½OZ LONG-GRAIN RICE

2 STICKS CELERY, SLICED

2 DRIED KAFFIR LIME LEAVES

4 SPRING ONIONS, SLICED

4 CUPS/1 LITRE/1¾ PINTS WATER

2 TABLESPOONS FISH SAUCE

½ TEASPOON SHRIMP PASTE, OPTIONAL

---

1. Remove any skin or bones from fish and cut fish into bite-sized pieces.
2. Heat oil in a large saucepan, add Green Curry Paste and turmeric, fry for 2 minutes.
3. Stir in all remaining ingredients except fish pieces and bring to the boil. Lower heat and simmer, covered with a lid, for 8 minutes.
4. Add fish pieces and cook for a further 4 minutes or until fish is cooked. Remove kaffir leaves and serve immediately as rice will soak up too much liquid if left to stand.
SERVES 4

Opposite: Rice Soup
Coconut and Chicken Soup

Fish Curry Soup

Thai-Style Pumpkin Soup

(A different and delicious way to
cook pumpkin.)
750G/1½LB PEELED PUMPKIN
1 TABLESPOON OIL
1½ TABLESPOONS RED CURRY PASTE (SEE PAGE 72)
2 ONIONS, CHOPPED
2 CUPS/500ML/16FL OZ COCONUT MILK
2 CUPS/500ML/16FL OZ CHICKEN STOCK

1. Cut pumpkin into bite-sized pieces. Heat oil in a large saucepan, add Red Curry Paste and onions and fry for 4 minutes.
2. Stir in pumpkin, coconut milk and chicken stock, bring to the boil. Lower heat and cover with a lid, simmer for 15 to 20 minutes or until pumpkin is tender. Don't overcook.
3. Purée half the soup in a blender or food processor and return to saucepan with un-processed soup and pumpkin. Heat and serve.
SERVES 6

Cabbage and Bamboo Shoot Soup

230G/7½OZ CAN BAMBOO SHOOTS
230G/7½OZ WATER CHESTNUTS
1 TABLESPOON OIL
2 CLOVES GARLIC, THINLY SLICED
200G/7OZ CHICKEN FILLETS, SLICED
6 CUPS/1.5 LITRES/2½ PINTS CHICKEN STOCK
2 CUPS/125G/4OZ SHREDDED CHINESE CABBAGE
2CM/¾IN CUBE PEELED FRESH GINGER, CHOPPED
1 RED CHILLI, SEEDED AND CHOPPED
1 TABLESPOON FISH SAUCE

1. Drain bamboo shoots and water chestnuts and rinse well. Slice both thinly.
2. Heat oil in a large saucepan, add garlic and sliced chicken and fry until chicken is golden.
3. Stir in all remaining ingredients and bring to the boil. Lower heat and simmer uncovered for 5 minutes.
SERVES 6

Pork and Noodle Soup

(If liked, sliced chicken can be used
in this soup instead of pork. It will be
equally delicious.)
4 CHINESE DRIED MUSHROOMS
1 TABLESPOON OIL
4 CLOVES GARLIC, FINELY SLICED
200G/7OZ LEAN PORK, SLICED
4 SPRING ONIONS, SLICED
6 CUPS/1.5 LITRES/2½ PINTS CHICKEN STOCK
1 CORIANDER PLANT, ROOTS INCLUDED, CHOPPED
2 TABLESPOONS FISH SAUCE
1 CUP/125G/4OZ BEAN SPROUTS
90G/3OZ DRIED ASIAN EGG NOODLES

1. Soak dried mushrooms in boiling water for 30 minutes. Drain and slice.
2. Heat oil in a large saucepan, add garlic and sliced pork and fry for 3 to 4 minutes. Stir in spring onions and mushrooms and fry for 2 minutes.
3. Add chicken stock, coriander, fish sauce, bean sprouts and noodles and bring to the boil. Lower heat, cover with a lid and simmer for 10 to 12 minutes or until noodles are cooked.
SERVES 4

Opposite: Cabbage and Bamboo Shoot Soup

Pork and Noodle Soup

Rice

The following recipes can be used as accompaniments to a main meal or the heartier rice dishes can be eaten as the main dish.

In Thailand, complex rice dishes are usually served as a lunch or dinner, and plain steamed rice is served with the main meal to complement the spicy or salty flavour of Thai food.

No Thai meal is complete without rice, Thailand's staple food. The most common type of rice used is long-grain rice which is usually steamed to produce long, fluffy, well-separated grains.

To steam rice for 2 to 3 people:

Place 1 cup/220g/7oz of rice in a saucepan with 2 cups/500ml/16fl oz water and bring to the boil. Cover pan with a lid, turn heat to very low and cook for 10 minutes. Remove pan from heat and allow to stand for 5 minutes. Remove lid and fluff rice with a fork, then serve. Alternatively, remove pan from heat and set aside undisturbed until ready to serve.

For larger quantities of rice use this guide:

1½ cups/330g/11oz rice cooked in 2½ cups/625ml/1 pint water serves 4 to 5 people.

2 cups/440g/14oz rice cooked in 3 cups/750ml/1¼ pints water serves 6 people.

Another method of cooking rice is to rapid boil. This method is ideal when a recipe calls for cooked rice. Simply bring a large saucepan of water to the boil, add rice gradually so that water does not go off the boil. Stir to separate grains and boil uncovered for 8 to 9 minutes or until rice is tender but still with some bite. Drain well and serve.

Cooked rice can be stored, covered, in the refrigerator for about 4 days and simply reheated over a pan of boiling water or, ideally, reheated in your microwave oven.

When cooking rice to use for fried rice or stir-frying, try to cook rice the day before. When cooked, drain well and spread into a shallow container, refrigerate until ready to serve.

RED CURRY RICE

2 TABLESPOONS OIL
1 CUP/220G/7OZ LONG-GRAIN RICE
1 TABLESPOON RED CURRY PASTE (SEE PAGE 72)
2 CORIANDER PLANTS, ROOTS INCLUDED, CHOPPED
2 CUPS/500ML/16FL OZ WATER
1½ TABLFSPOONS SOY SAUCE

1. Heat oil in a large saucepan. Add rice and fry until golden brown, about 4 minutes, stirring occasionally. Stir in curry paste and fry for 1 minute.
2. Add coriander, water and soy sauce and bring to the boil. Cover with a lid, turn heat to very low and cook for 10 minutes. Remove from heat and allow to stand for 5 minutes before serving.
SERVES 4

Red Curry Rice

21

Prawns with Basil and Rice

2 TABLESPOONS OIL

1 EGG, LIGHTLY BEATEN

1 ONION, CHOPPED

2 CLOVES GARLIC, CHOPPED

2 TEASPOONS SHRIMP PASTE

1 LARGE TOMATO, CHOPPED

2 SPRING ONIONS, SLICED

2 TABLESPOONS OYSTER SAUCE

5 CUPS/925G/32OZ COOKED LONG-GRAIN RICE

15 FRESH BASIL LEAVES

375G/12OZ COOKED PRAWNS, PEELED

1. Heat 1 tablespoon of the oil in a large frying pan. Add beaten egg and cook 1 to 2 minutes each side, remove from pan and cut into thin strips.
2. Heat remaining 1 tablespoon oil in pan, add onion and garlic and fry for 2 minutes. Stir in shrimp paste, mixing well.
3. Add all remaining ingredients and cook for 2 to 3 minutes, stirring occasionally. Serve topped with the sliced egg.
SERVES 4 TO 6

Coconut Rice

2 TABLESPOONS BUTTER

1 CUP/220G/7OZ LONG-GRAIN RICE

1¾ CUPS/430ML/14FL OZ COCONUT MILK

1 STALK LEMON GRASS, THINLY SLICED

1CM/½IN CUBE PEELED FRESH GINGER, CHOPPED

2 TABLESPOONS FISH SAUCE

2 TABLESPOONS FINELY CHOPPED PEANUTS

1. Melt butter in a large saucepan. Add rice and fry over a moderate heat until golden brown.
2. Add all remaining ingredients except peanuts and bring to the boil. Turn heat to very low, cover with a lid and cook for 10 minutes. Remove from heat and stand for 5 minutes, fluff rice with a fork and serve sprinkled with chopped peanuts.
SERVES 4

Garlic Rice with Tangy Chicken

Garlic Rice

1 TABLESPOON OIL

4 CLOVES GARLIC, CHOPPED

1½ CUPS/330G/11OZ LONG-GRAIN RICE

2½ CUPS/625ML/1 PINT CHICKEN STOCK

Tangy Chicken

1 TABLESPOON OIL

1 ONION, SLICED

1CM/½IN CUBE PEELED FRESH GINGER, SLICED

250G/8OZ (½LB) CHICKEN FILLETS, SLICED

1 TABLESPOON BROWN SUGAR, WELL PACKED

1 TABLESPOON TAMARIND SAUCE

1 TABLESPOON FISH SAUCE

½ CUP/125ML/4FL OZ CHICKEN STOCK

1. *Garlic Rice:* Heat oil in a large saucepan, add garlic and fry for 1 minute over a moderate heat. Add rice and fry for 2 minutes.
2. Stir in chicken stock and bring to the boil. Turn heat to very low, cover with a lid and cook for 10 minutes. Spoon into an oven-proof serving dish with a lid and keep warm in a low oven.
3. *Tangy Chicken:* Heat oil in a saucepan or frying pan, add onion, ginger and sliced chicken and fry for 5 minutes or until chicken is golden brown.
4. Stir in sugar, tamarind sauce, fish sauce and chicken stock, bring to the boil, lower heat and simmer for 4 to 5 minutes or until sauce is reduced by about one-third (there should still be a good quantity of sauce left). Spoon chicken and sauce over rice and serve.
SERVES 4

Opposite: Prawns with Basil And Rice

Garlic Rice With Tangy Chicken

SPICED RICE

1 TABLESPOON BUTTER

1 ONION, CHOPPED

1 RED OR GREEN CHILLI, SEEDED AND CHOPPED

1 TEASPOON CUMIN SEEDS

1 TABLESPOON FISH SAUCE

1 CUP/220G/7OZ LONG-GRAIN RICE

2 CUPS/500ML/16FL OZ WATER

1. Melt butter in a large saucepan. Add onion, chilli and cumin seeds and fry over a moderate heat for 3 to 4 minutes.

2. Stir in fish sauce, rice and water and bring to the boil. Turn heat to very low, cover with a lid and cook for 10 minutes. Remove from heat and stand for 5 minutes. Fluff with a fork and serve.

SERVES 4

THAI FRIED RICE

(This fried rice is great when entertaining a crowd. It serves 8 as a main meal or 10 to 12 with other dishes at a party. The recipe is easily doubled or halved.)

2 TABLESPOONS OIL

4 CLOVES GARLIC, CRUSHED

400G/13OZ LEAN PORK, CHOPPED

2 RED OR GREEN CAPSICUMS (PEPPERS), CHOPPED

4 SPRING ONIONS, CHOPPED

4 TABLESPOONS FISH SAUCE

4 TABLESPOONS TOMATO SAUCE

375G/12OZ COOKED PRAWNS, PEELED

8 CUPS/1.5KG/3LB COOKED LONG-GRAIN RICE

2 EGGS, LIGHTLY BEATEN

1. Heat oil in a large frying pan. Add garlic and pork and fry until pork is golden brown.

2. Add capsicum, spring onions, fish sauce, tomato sauce, prawns and rice, cook over a moderate heat for 3 minutes.

3. Stir in beaten eggs and mix lightly through. Cover with a lid and cook for 2 to 3 minutes, stirring once or twice.

SERVES 8

Opposite: Thai Fried Rice

Spiced Rice

Fish and Seafood

Seafood with Chilli and Basil

16 MUSSELS IN THE SHELL
250G/8OZ (½LB) CLEANED CALAMARI (SQUID)
1 TABLESPOON OIL
2 CLOVES GARLIC, CHOPPED
6 SPRING ONIONS, SLICED
20 FRESH BASIL LEAVES
2 TABLESPOONS FISH SAUCE
1 TABLESPOON SOY SAUCE
1 RED OR GREEN CHILLI, SEEDED AND CHOPPED
1 TABLESPOON BROWN SUGAR
200G/7OZ PEELED RAW PRAWNS

1. Scrub mussels and remove any grit or beard, rinse well. Score calamari all over in a criss-cross pattern, then cut into pieces about 2cm x 3cm/¾in x 1¼in.
2. Heat oil in a large saucepan. Add garlic and spring onions and fry for 1 minute. Add all remaining ingredients except calamari and prawns and cook, covered with a lid, for 6 minutes.
3. Stir in calamari and prawns and cook a further 3 to 4 minutes or until prawns and calamari are cooked. Serve immediately.
SERVES 4

Mussels with Ginger and Bamboo Shoots

1.5KG/3LB MUSSELS IN THE SHELL
230G/7½OZ CAN BAMBOO SHOOTS
1 TABLESPOON OIL
6 SPRING ONIONS, SLICED
4CM/1½IN CUBE PEELED FRESH GINGER, CUT INTO THIN STRIPS
3 STALKS LEMON GRASS, SLICED
3 DRIED KAFFIR LEAVES
1 RED CHILLI, SEEDED AND SLICED
3 TABLESPOONS FISH SAUCE
1 CUP/250ML/8FL OZ WATER

1. Scrub mussels and remove any grit or beard, rinse well. Drain bamboo shoots, rinse well and cut into strips.
2. Heat oil in a large saucepan. Add spring onions, ginger, lemon grass, kaffir leaves and chilli and fry for 2 minutes.
3. Add mussels, bamboo shoots, fish sauce and water and cover with a lid. Bring to the boil, lower heat and simmer for 15 minutes; any mussels that do not open should be discarded. Serve in bowls so that the liquid can be enjoyed after the mussels are eaten.
SERVES 4

Mussels with Ginger and Bamboo Shoots

Seafood with Chilli and Basil

Prawns in Coconut Milk

500G/1LB RAW PRAWNS

1 TABLESPOON OIL

1 ONION, CHOPPED

1 RED CHILLI, SEEDED AND CHOPPED

1 TEASPOON CORNFLOUR

1 CUP/250ML/8FL OZ COCONUT MILK

2 STALKS LEMON GRASS

4 DRIED KAFFIR LEAVES

1 TABLESPOON FISH SAUCE

½ CUP/60G/2OZ SLICED GREEN BEANS

1. Peel prawns and devein. Heat oil in a saucepan. Add onion and chilli and fry for 2 minutes.
2. Mix cornflour and coconut milk together until smooth, add to pan with lemon grass, kaffir leaves and fish sauce. Cook, stirring, until sauce boils and thickens. Lower heat and simmer for 2 minutes.
3. Stir in prawns and beans and cook a further 2 to 3 minutes or until prawns are just cooked. Remove kaffir leaves and serve with steamed long-grain rice.
SERVES 4

Calamari with Mint

500G/1LB CLEANED CALAMARI (SQUID) TUBES

2 TABLESPOONS OIL

5 CLOVES GARLIC, FINELY CHOPPED

50 FRESH MINT LEAVES

2 TABLESPOONS WATER

2 TABLESPOONS FISH SAUCE

200G/7OZ SNOW PEAS (MANGETOUT), TRIMMED

CRACKED BLACK PEPPER

1. Slice calamari into thin rings and pat dry.
2. Heat oil in a large frying pan. Add garlic and fry over a high heat for 30 seconds. Add calamari and fry for 2 minutes, stirring occasionally.
3. Add mint leaves, water, fish sauce and snow peas and cook for 1 to 2 minutes. Serve immediately, sprinkled with cracked black pepper.
SERVES 4

Hot Chilli Prawns

500G/1LB RAW PRAWNS

2 TABLESPOONS OIL

1 ONION, HALVED AND SLICED

2 TABLESPOONS RED CURRY PASTE (SEE PAGE 72)

1 TABLESPOON BROWN SUGAR

2 TABLESPOONS CHOPPED FRESH CORIANDER

1. Peel prawns, leaving tails intact, and devein.
2. Heat oil and fry onion for 1 minute. Add curry paste and fry for a further 1 minute.
3. Stir in prawns and brown sugar and fry over a moderate heat until prawns are cooked, stirring occasionally. Serve immediately, sprinkled with chopped coriander.
SERVES 4

Green Curry of Fish

(Fresh basil can be used instead of dried in this recipe. You will need about 8 fresh leaves. Keep them whole.)

500G/1LB WHITE FISH FILLETS

1 TABLESPOON VEGETABLE OIL

2 TABLESPOONS GREEN CURRY PASTE (SEE PAGE 72)

½ TEASPOON DRIED BASIL LEAVES

3 DRIED KAFFIR LEAVES

1 CUP/250ML/8FL OZ COCONUT MILK

2 TABLESPOONS FISH SAUCE

2 STRIPS LEMON PEEL, ABOUT 5CM/2IN LONG

1 TABLESPOON BROWN SUGAR, WELL PACKED

1. Remove any skin or bones from fish and cut into large bite-sized chunks.
2. Heat oil in a saucepan, add curry paste, basil and kaffir leaves and fry for 3 minutes, stirring. Stir in coconut milk, fish sauce, lemon peel and brown sugar and bring to the boil. Lower heat and simmer for 4 minutes.
3. Add fish pieces and simmer, uncovered, for 4 to 5 minutes or until fish is cooked. Remove kaffir leaves and serve with steamed long-grain rice.
SERVES 4

Opposite: Calamari With Mint
Hot Chilli Prawns

SWEET AND SOUR THAI FISH

1 WHOLE FISH, SNAPPER OR BREAM,
ABOUT 1.25KG/2¼LB

¼ CUP/30G/1OZ FLOUR

OIL FOR FRYING

SWEET AND SOUR SAUCE

2 CLOVES GARLIC, CHOPPED

1 ONION, CHOPPED

1 TOMATO, CHOPPED

1 CARROT, SLICED

2CM/¾IN CUBE PEELED FRESH GINGER

¼ CUP/60G/2OZ BROWN SUGAR, WELL PACKED

2 TABLESPOONS FISH SAUCE

¼ CUP/60ML/2FL OZ WHITE VINEGAR

2 TEASPOONS CORNFLOUR

⅓ CUP/80ML/2½FL OZ WATER

1. Clean and scale fish and wash well. Pat dry with absorbent paper. Make about 4 diagonal cuts on each side of the fish down to the bone. Coat lightly in flour, shaking off any excess.
2. Heat oil in a wok or frying pan and deep-fry the fish until golden brown and crisp on both sides. Drain on absorbent paper and keep warm.
3. *Sweet and Sour Sauce:* Pour off most of oil from pan, leaving 2 tablespoons and heat. Add garlic and onion and fry for 2 minutes. Stir in remaining vegetables and ginger, brown sugar, fish sauce and vinegar.
4. Mix together cornflour and water, add to pan and continue stirring until sauce boils and thickens. Lower heat and simmer until vegetables are tender but still crunchy, about 2 minutes. Serve sauce spooned over fish.
SERVES 4

CRISPY FISH IN CHILLI SAUCE

(Thai Sweet Chilli Sauce is available at Asian food shops or some supermarkets. It is sweet and has the chilli seeds left in.)

500G/1LB WHITE FISH FILLETS

½ CUP/60G/2OZ FLOUR

OIL FOR FRYING

CHILLI SAUCE

2 ONIONS, CHOPPED

2 CLOVES GARLIC, CRUSHED

2 TABLESPOONS BROWN SUGAR, WELL PACKED

2 TABLESPOONS FISH SAUCE

2 TABLESPOONS THAI SWEET CHILLI SAUCE

½ CUP/125ML/4FL OZ WATER

1. Remove any skin and bones from fish and discard. Slice fish into 1cm/½in-thick strips and coat lightly in flour, shaking off any excess.
2. Heat about 1cm/½in oil in a large frying pan. Add fish strips to pan in batches and fry until golden brown all over, drain on absorbent paper and keep warm.
3. *Chilli Sauce:* Pour most of oil from pan, leaving about 1 tablespoon. Add onions and garlic and fry for 3 minutes. Stir in remaining sauce ingredients and bring to the boil. Lower heat and simmer for about 3 to 4 minutes or until sauce is slightly syrupy.
4. Place fish on a serving plate and spoon sauce over. Serve immediately.
SERVES 4

Crispy Fish in Chilli Sauce

Opposite: Sweet and Sour Thai Fish

Beef
and Lamb

CHILLI BEEF

2 TO 3 RED CHILLIES, SEEDED

1 ONION, PEELED AND QUARTERED

3 CLOVES GARLIC, PEELED

3 TABLESPOONS OIL

500G/1LB RUMP OR TOPSIDE BEEF, THINLY SLICED

1 TABLESPOON OYSTER SAUCE

2 TABLESPOONS FISH SAUCE

4 TABLESPOONS WATER

1 RED CAPSICUM (PEPPER), SLICED

2 TABLESPOONS CHOPPED FRESH CORIANDER

1. Place chillies, onion and garlic into a food processor or blender and purée until almost smooth.
2. Heat 2 tablespoons of the oil in a wok or large frying pan. Fry meat until well browned (you may have to do this in batches) and set aside.
3. Add remaining 1 tablespoon oil to pan and stir-fry chilli paste over a moderate heat for 4 minutes or until golden brown.
4. Stir in beef, oyster sauce, fish sauce, water and capsicum and fry for a further 2 minutes or until meat is cooked. Serve sprinkled with chopped coriander.
SERVES 4

BEEF ON A BED OF GREENS

(Bok choy is an Asian vegetable with lovely white, crunchy stems and green leafy tops. It is available at some fruit and vegetable shops and Asian food shops. If unavailable, substitute fresh young silverbeet.)

4 CHINESE DRIED MUSHROOMS

8 TO 10 STALKS BOK CHOY

2 TABLESPOONS OIL

4 CLOVES GARLIC, CHOPPED

500G/1LB LEAN STEAK, THINLY SLICED

4 SPRING ONIONS, CUT INTO 3CM LENGTHS

2 TABLESPOONS OYSTER SAUCE

⅓ CUP/80ML/2½FL OZ WATER

1 TEASPOON SUGAR

1. Soak mushrooms in hot water for 30 minutes, drain and slice thinly. Wash bok choy well and cut into 5cm/2in lengths including green tops.
2. Heat 1 tablespoon of the oil in a wok or large frying pan. Add bok choy and stir-fry for 2 to 3 minutes or until tender but still crunchy. Spoon onto a serving plate and keep warm.
3. Tip off any liquid in pan and add remaining 1 tablespoon oil to pan. Fry garlic and beef until well browned.
4. Stir in all remaining ingredients including mushrooms and cook for a further 2 minutes. Spoon over bok choy and serve.
SERVES 4

Beef on a Bed of Greens

Chilli Beef

Thai Meatballs with Peanut Sauce

500G/1LB TOPSIDE MINCE

FLOUR FOR COATING

OIL FOR FRYING

2 TABLESPOONS CHOPPED FRESH CORIANDER

PEANUT SAUCE

1 TABLESPOON RED CURRY PASTE (SEE PAGE 72)

2 TABLESPOONS CRUNCHY PEANUT BUTTER

1 TABLESPOON BROWN SUGAR, WELL PACKED

1 TABLESPOON LEMON JUICE

1¼ CUPS/310ML/10FL OZ COCONUT MILK

1. Roll beef mince into small balls and coat lightly in flour. Deep- or shallow-fry meatballs until golden brown and cooked through. Drain on absorbent paper.
2. *Peanut Sauce:* Drain off most of oil from pan, leaving about 1 tablespoon. Add curry paste and fry for 1 minute.
3. Add all other ingredients except coriander and bring to the boil. Add meatballs, lower heat and simmer for 5 minutes or until sauce has thickened. Sprinkle with coriander to serve.
SERVES 4

Lamb with Mint

1 MEDIUM EGGPLANT (AUBERGINE)

1 TABLESPOON SALT

2 TABLESPOONS OIL

500G/1LB LEAN LAMB, THINLY SLICED

2 CLOVES GARLIC, CHOPPED

1 RED CHILLI, SEEDED AND CHOPPED

2 TABLESPOONS FISH SAUCE

1 TABLESPOON BROWN SUGAR, WELL PACKED

⅓ CUP/80ML/2½FL OZ WATER

20 FRESH MINT LEAVES

1. Cut eggplant into bite-sized chunks, place in a colander and sprinkle with salt, mix well and leave to drain for 20 minutes. Rinse under cold water and drain well.
2. Heat oil in a wok or large frying pan. Add lamb and garlic and fry until well browned (you may need to do this in batches). Add eggplant and chilli and stir-fry over a moderate heat for 5 minutes.
3. Stir in fish sauce, brown sugar, water and mint leaves and fry for a further 1 minute or until eggplant is softened. If sauce becomes too thick, add a little extra water. Serve with steamed long-grain rice.
SERVES 4

Opposite: Lamb with Mint

Thai Meatballs with Peanut Sauce

CHILLI SAUCE MEATLOAF

(Meatloaf is not traditionally Thai but using Thai ingredients gives the humble meatloaf a wonderful flavour. Thai Sweet Chilli Sauce is available in Asian food shops or at some supermarkets or use the recipe on page 8.)

MEATLOAF

750G/1½LB TOPSIDE MINCE

1 ONION, FINELY CHOPPED

2 CLOVES GARLIC, CHOPPED

230G/7½OZ CAN WATER CHESTNUTS, WASHED, DRAINED AND CHOPPED

1 CUP/185G/6OZ COOKED LONG-GRAIN RICE

1 CORIANDER PLANT, CHOPPED

2 TABLESPOONS TOMATO SAUCE

1 EGG, LIGHTLY BEATEN

CHILLI GLAZE

3 TABLESPOONS THAI SWEET CHILLI SAUCE

1 TABLESPOON BROWN SUGAR, WELL PACKED

1. Mix all meatloaf ingredients together in a large bowl. Press mixture into a well-greased 12cm x 22cm/5in x 9in loaf tin and bake in a moderate oven for 50 minutes.
2. Mix Sweet Chilli Sauce and brown sugar together and spoon over meatloaf. Return to oven for a further 15 minutes or until meatloaf is cooked. Serve sliced.
SERVES 6 TO 8

Chilli Sauce Meatloaf

MUSLIM BEEF CURRY

1 TABLESPOON OIL

2 TABLESPOONS MUSLIM CURRY PASTE (SEE PAGE 72)

1KG/2LB ROUND STEAK, CUBED

3 ONIONS, QUARTERED

3 CUPS/750ML/1¼ PINTS COCONUT MILK

2 TABLESPOONS BROWN SUGAR, WELL PACKED

1 TABLESPOON FISH SAUCE

1 TABLESPOON TAMARIND SAUCE

2 POTATOES, PEELED AND CUT INTO CHUNKS

½ CUP/90G/3OZ PEANUTS

1. Heat oil in a large saucepan, add curry paste and fry for 1 minute.
2. Stir in beef, onions, coconut milk, brown sugar, fish sauce and tamarind sauce and bring to the boil. Lower heat and simmer for 20 minutes.
3. Add potatoes and peanuts and cook a further 20 to 25 minutes or until potatoes are cooked and beef is tender. Serve with steamed long-grain rice.
SERVES 8

RED CURRY OF BEEF

1 TABLESPOON OIL

2 TABLESPOONS RED CURRY PASTE (SEE PAGE 72)

1KG/2LB CHUCK STEAK, CUBED

1¾ CUPS/430ML/14FL OZ COCONUT MILK

2 TABLESPOONS FISH SAUCE

4 DRIED KAFFIR LEAVES

15 FRESH BASIL LEAVES OR 2 TEASPOONS DRIED

1. Heat oil in a wok or large frying pan. Add curry paste and fry for 1 minute. Stir in all remaining ingredients and bring to the boil.
2. Lower heat and simmer for 1½ hours or until beef is tender. Remove kaffir leaves and serve with steamed long-grain rice.
SERVES 6

Opposite: Muslim Beef Curry

Thai Beef Salad

250g/8oz (½lb) fillet steak

cracked black pepper

1 to 2 tablespoons oil

lettuce or salad greens

Dressing

3 tablespoons lemon juice

1 tablespoon brown sugar, well packed

1 coriander plant, chopped

1 red chilli, seeded and sliced

½ small onion, thinly sliced

1. Remove any fat from steak and sprinkle both sides with pepper, pressing on firmly. Heat oil in a frying pan and fry steak over a high heat until well browned on both sides and still rare in the centre. Remove from pan and slice thinly.
2. Mix all dressing ingredients together and pour over sliced beef. Arrange on a platter with lettuce or salad greens and serve while warm.
Serves 4

Beef with Fresh Basil and Beans

200g/7oz green beans or snake beans

1 tablespoon oil

3 cloves garlic, chopped

250g/8oz (½lb) oyster blade steak, thinly sliced

30 fresh basil leaves

2 tablespoons fish sauce

2 tablespoons water

1. Top and tail beans and cut into 5cm/2in lengths.
2. Heat oil in a wok or large frying pan, add garlic and beef and fry until beef is well browned. Add basil leaves and beans and stir-fry for 1 minute.
3. Add fish sauce and water and fry a further 1 minute or until beans are cooked but still very crunchy. Serve with steamed long-grain rice.
Serves 4

Sweet Lamb with Coriander

2 red chillies

2 coriander plants

oil for deep-frying

500g/1lb lean sliced lamb

1 onion, thinly sliced

1 tablespoon soy sauce

¼ cup/60g/2oz brown sugar, well packed

¼ cup/60ml/2fl oz water

1. Seed chillies and slice thickly. Cut coriander stem and roots into 3cm/1¼in lengths and tear green tops into large sprigs. Heat oil in a saucepan and deep-fry chillies and coriander until crisp and drain on absorbent paper.
2. Heat 1 tablespoon oil in a wok or large frying pan. Add lamb and onion and fry until lamb is well browned.
3. Stir in soy sauce, brown sugar and water. Lower heat and stir-fry over a moderate heat for 5 minutes or until sauce is syrupy and lamb is cooked. If sauce becomes too dry add a little water. Serve sprinkled with deep-fried chilli and coriander.
Serves 4

Opposite: Beef with Fresh Basil and Beans
Sweet Lamb with Coriander

Thai Beef Salad

Pork

Red Roast Pork

750g/1½lb pork fillet

Marinade

½ teaspoon red food colouring

2 tablespoons water

3 cloves garlic, crushed

1 tablespoon fish sauce

1 tablespoon soy sauce

1 tablespoon oyster sauce

1 tablespoon brown sugar

2cm/¾in cube peeled fresh ginger, grated

½ teaspoon Chinese five-spice powder

1. Remove any fat from pork and place pork into a shallow dish.
2. Mix all marinade ingredients together in a bowl and pour over pork. Using rubber gloves, mix pork and marinade together until well coated. Cover and refrigerate for 2 to 3 hours or overnight.
3. Drain marinade from pork and place pork on a wire rack over a baking dish. Cook in a hot oven (200°C/400°F) for 10 minutes. Baste with marinade and lower heat to 180°C/350°F. Cook for a further 20 to 30 minutes or until pork is cooked.
4. Remove from oven and stand for 10 minutes. Slice thinly and serve with steamed long-grain rice or add to noodle dishes or soups.
Serves 4 to 6

Spicy Mint Pork

750g/1½lb pork spare ribs

salt

1 tablespoon oil

1 tablespoon fish sauce

1 tablespoon lemon juice

2 tablespoons chopped mint

2 tablespoons chopped coriander

2 teaspoons brown sugar

3 spring onions, finely chopped

½ red chilli, seeded and finely chopped

lettuce leaves

1. Remove skin from spare ribs, rub with a little salt and cook under a hot griller until golden brown and crackling. Cool and break into small pieces.
2. Cut remaining pork into small pieces, discarding any excess fat. Process pork meat in a food processor or blender until minced. Heat oil and fry mince until golden brown and crumbly.
3. Add all remaining ingredients except lettuce and toss together. Remove from heat and serve on a bed of lettuce or in individual lettuce cups topped with crackling.
Serves 4

Red Roast Pork

Spicy Mint Pork

Pork Omelette

(This omelette is delicious served with a
Sweet Chilli Sauce, see page 8.)

2 TABLESPOONS OIL
125G/4OZ MINCED PORK
2 CLOVES GARLIC, CHOPPED
1 TABLESPOON SOY SAUCE
½ CUP/125ML/4FL OZ WATER
4 EGGS, LIGHTLY BEATEN
3 SPRING ONIONS, CHOPPED
1 CORIANDER PLANT, ROOTS INCLUDED, CHOPPED

1. Heat 1 tablespoon of the oil in a large
frying pan, add pork and garlic and fry until
pork is golden brown and crumbly.
2. Add soy sauce and water and bring to the
boil. Lower heat and simmer until all liquid
has evaporated. Remove pork from pan and
set aside.
3. Wash and dry pan and return to heat, add
remaining 1 tablespoon oil, swirling to coat.
Pour in beaten eggs to coat base of pan.
4. Top with pork, spring onions and coriander
and cover with a lid. Cook over a moderate
heat until egg is beginning to set. Fold one
half of omelette over and continue cooking
until egg is cooked in the centre. Serve cut
into wedges.
SERVES 4

Pork Spare Ribs with Peanut Sauce

1KG/2LB PORK SPARE RIBS
2 CLOVES GARLIC, CRUSHED
2 TABLESPOONS FISH SAUCE
2 TEASPOONS BROWN SUGAR
1 RED CHILLI, SEEDED AND FINELY CHOPPED
1 CORIANDER PLANT, CHOPPED

Peanut Sauce

½ CUP/90G/3OZ PEANUTS
1 TABLESPOON OIL
1 ONION, FINELY CHOPPED
¾ CUP/180ML/6FL OZ WATER
1 TABLESPOON FISH SAUCE
2 TEASPOONS BROWN SUGAR
1 TABLESPOON LEMON JUICE

1. Cut spare ribs in half and place in a shallow dish with garlic, fish sauce, brown sugar
and chilli and mix well. Refrigerate for 2 to
3 hours.
2. *Peanut Sauce:* Chop peanuts very finely in
a food processor or blender.
3. Heat oil and fry onion for 3 to 4 minutes. Add
peanuts and all remaining sauce ingredients
except coriander and bring to the boil. Lower
heat and simmer for 3 to 4 minutes or until
sauce has thickened.
4. Cook spare ribs on a barbecue or in a moderate oven until well browned and cooked
through. Serve with Peanut Sauce, sprinkle
with chopped coriander.
SERVES 4 TO 6

Opposite: Pork Spare Ribs with Peanut Sauce

Pork Omelette

Pork with Broccoli and Mint

2 TABLESPOONS OIL

500G/1LB LEAN PORK, SLICED

2 CLOVES GARLIC, CHOPPED

1 TABLESPOON FISH SAUCE

1 TABLESPOON OYSTER SAUCE

1 TABLESPOON WATER

1 TEASPOON BROWN SUGAR

1 GREEN CHILLI, SEEDED AND SLICED

250G/8OZ (½LB) BROCCOLI,
BROKEN INTO FLORETS

20 FRESH MINT LEAVES

1. Heat oil in a wok or large frying pan. Add
pork and garlic and fry until pork is golden.
2. Add fish sauce, oyster sauce, water, brown
sugar, chilli and broccoli and bring to the boil.
Lower heat and stir-fry for 2 to 3 minutes or
until broccoli is cooked but still crunchy.
3. Add mint, toss through and serve.
SERVES 4

Barbecued Spare Ribs with Sweet Sauce

1KG/2LB PORK SPARE RIBS

<u>SAUCE</u>

½ CUCUMBER

2 TABLESPOONS OIL

1 ONION, CHOPPED

⅓ CUP/80ML/2½FL OZ TOMATO SAUCE

2 TABLESPOONS FISH SAUCE

1 TABLESPOON WHITE VINEGAR

2 TABLESPOONS BROWN SUGAR, WELL PACKED

½ RED CHILLI, SEEDED AND CHOPPED

1. Place spare ribs in a large saucepan, cover
with water and bring to the boil. Lower heat
and simmer for 20 minutes. Remove from
heat and drain well. Refrigerate until ready
to barbecue.
2. *Sauce:* Cut cucumber in half lengthwise,
remove seeds and slice. Heat oil in a saucepan,
add onion and fry for 3 minutes. Add all other
sauce ingredients except cucumber and bring
to the boil. Lower heat and simmer for 1 minute.
Add cucumber and cook for a further 1 minute.
3. Cook spare ribs over hot coals on a barbecue until golden brown all over. Spoon
sauce over and serve.
SERVES 4 TO 6

*Barbecued Spare Ribs
with Sweet Sauce*

Opposite: Pork with Broccoli and Mint

PEPPER PORK

2 TABLESPOONS OIL

500G/1LB LEAN PORK, THINLY SLICED

½ TEASPOON FRESHLY GROUND BLACK PEPPER

3 CLOVES GARLIC, CHOPPED

1 ONION, CHOPPED

2 TABLESPOONS OYSTER SAUCE

¼ CUP/60ML/2FL OZ WATER

1 TEASPOON BROWN SUGAR

125G/4OZ SNOW PEAS (MANGETOUT), TRIMMED

1. Heat oil in a wok or large frying pan. Add pork, pepper, garlic and onion and fry until pork is golden brown and cooked.
2. Stir in oyster sauce, water, brown sugar and snow peas and stir-fry for 1 minute. Serve with steamed long-grain rice.
SERVES 4

SWEET CHILLI PORK

2 TABLESPOONS OIL

2 ONIONS, THINLY SLICED

1 RED CHILLI, SEEDED AND CHOPPED

500G/1LB LEAN PORK, THINLY SLICED

½ CUP/100G/3½OZ BROWN SUGAR, LIGHTLY PACKED

½ CUP/125ML/4FL OZ WATER

1 TABLESPOON FISH SAUCE

1 CORIANDER PLANT, CHOPPED

1. Heat oil in a wok or large frying pan. Add onions, chilli and pork and fry until golden brown, about 5 minutes.
2. Add brown sugar, water and fish sauce and bring to the boil. Lower heat and simmer for 4 to 5 minutes or until sauce is thick and syrupy, stirring while cooking. Sprinkle with chopped coriander and serve with steamed long-grain rice.
SERVES 4

Opposite: Pepper Pork

Sweet Chilli Pork

Chicken

CHICKEN WITH CRISP CHILLI AND CASHEWS

3 TABLESPOONS OIL

4 FRESH RED CHILLIES, SEEDED AND SLICED

3 CLOVES GARLIC, SLICED

500G/1LB CHICKEN FILLETS, SLICED

1 ONION, SLICED

1 TABLESPOON OYSTER SAUCE

1 TABLESPOON FISH SAUCE

1 TABLESPOON TAMARIND SAUCE

2 TABLESPOONS WATER

2 TEASPOONS BROWN SUGAR

½ CUP/90G/3OZ ROASTED CASHEW NUTS

1. Heat 2 tablespoons of the oil in a wok or frying pan, add chillies and garlic and fry until crisp and golden, drain on absorbent paper.
2. Add remaining 1 tablespoon of oil to pan and fry chicken and onion until chicken is golden brown and cooked.
3. Stir in sauces, water and brown sugar and stir-fry for 2 minutes. Add cashews and mix through. Serve topped with fried chilli and garlic.
SERVES 4

CURRY OF CHICKEN WITH POTATOES

750G/1½LB CHICKEN PIECES, E.G. DRUMSTICKS, HALF BREASTS, THIGHS

1 TABLESPOON OIL

2 TABLESPOONS RED CURRY PASTE (SEE PAGE 72)

2 CUPS/500ML/16FL OZ COCONUT MILK

1 ONION, QUARTERED

1 LARGE POTATO, CUT INTO 2CM/¾IN CUBES

1 TABLESPOON FISH SAUCE

3 DRIED KAFFIR LEAVES

¾ CUP/90G/3OZ PEAS

1. Remove skin from chicken pieces and discard.
2. Heat oil in a large saucepan, add curry paste and fry for 1 minute. Add chicken pieces and fry a further 2 minutes, tossing so the curry paste coats the chicken.
3. Stir in all remaining ingredients except peas and bring to the boil. Lower heat and simmer, uncovered, for 30 minutes.
4. Add peas and simmer a further 5 minutes or until chicken and peas are cooked. Remove kaffir leaves before serving.
SERVES 4

Chicken with Crisp Chilli and Cashews

Curry of Chicken with Potatoes

BARBECUED GARLIC CHICKEN

(This marinade is also ideal for quail.)
1KG/2LB CHICKEN PIECES

MARINADE

6 CLOVES GARLIC, CRUSHED
¼ CUP/60ML/2FL OZ LEMON JUICE
2 TABLESPOONS THAI SWEET CHILLI SAUCE
(SEE NOTE)
1 CORIANDER PLANT, CHOPPED
1 TABLESPOON BROWN SUGAR
2 TEASPOONS SOY SAUCE

1. Wash chicken pieces and pat dry. Place in a large dish.
2. *Marinade:* Mix all marinade ingredients together in a bowl. Pour mixture over chicken pieces and mix until all pieces are well coated with marinade. Cover and refrigerate for 2 to 3 hours.
3. Barbecue chicken pieces over glowing coals until golden brown all over and cooked through.
Note: Sweet Chilli Sauce is available in bottles in Asian food shops or some supermarkets. It is usually called Thai Sweet Chilli Sauce. If preferred, you can make the recipe on page 8.
SERVES 4

CHICKEN IN COCONUT MILK

1KG/2LB CHICKEN PIECES, E.G. DRUMSTICKS,
THIGHS, HALF BREASTS
1 ONION, CHOPPED
2 CUPS/500ML/16FL OZ COCONUT MILK
4 DRIED KAFFIR LEAVES
2CM/¾IN CUBE PEELED FRESH GINGER, CHOPPED
1 GREEN CHILLI, SEEDED AND CHOPPED
2 TABLESPOONS LEMON JUICE
2 TABLESPOONS FISH SAUCE
2 TEASPOONS BROWN SUGAR
⅓ CUP/60G/2OZ PEANUTS, ROUGHLY CHOPPED

1. Remove skin from chicken pieces and discard. Place chicken pieces into a large saucepan.
2. Add all remaining ingredients and bring to the boil. Lower heat and simmer uncovered for 30 to 35 minutes or until chicken is cooked. Remove kaffir leaves and discard. Serve with steamed long-grain rice.
SERVES 4

Opposite: Barbecued Garlic Chicken

Chicken in Coconut Milk

PEPPERY QUAIL

4 QUAIL

3 TABLESPOONS FISH SAUCE

MARINADE

2 CORIANDER PLANTS, CHOPPED

4 CLOVES GARLIC, PEELED

1 TEASPOON CRACKED BLACK PEPPER

1 TABLESPOON OIL

1. Wash and pat dry quail and cut into halves. Place into a large shallow dish. Pour fish sauce over quail.
2. *Marinade:* Place all marinade ingredients in a food processor or blender and process until mixture is very finely chopped. Spread all over quail and refrigerate covered for 2 to 3 hours.
3. Barbecue quail halves over glowing coals on a barbecue until golden brown on both sides and cooked through. Serve with Sweet Chilli Sauce. (See page 8.)
SERVES 4

CREAMY PEANUT CHICKEN

1 TABLESPOON OIL

1 TABLESPOON RED CURRY PASTE (SEE PAGE 72)

500G/1LB CHICKEN FILLETS, CUT INTO SMALL CUBES

1 CUP/250ML/8FL OZ COCONUT MILK

1 TABLESPOON FISH SAUCE

1 TABLESPOON BROWN SUGAR

¼ CUP/60G/2OZ CRUNCHY PEANUT BUTTER

LEMON WEDGES

1. Heat oil in a wok or frying pan, add curry paste and fry for 1 minute. Stir in chicken and fry for 4 to 5 minutes or until golden brown.
2. Add all remaining ingredients except lemon wedges and bring to the boil. Lower heat and simmer uncovered for 10 to 12 minutes or until sauce has thickened.
3. Serve with steamed long-grain rice and lemon wedges.
SERVES 4

Opposite: Peppery Quail

Creamy Peanut Chicken

CHICKEN WITH BASIL AND BROCCOLI

1 TABLESPOON OIL

2 CLOVES GARLIC, CHOPPED

500G/1LB CHICKEN THIGH FILLETS, SLICED

1 RED CHILLI, SEEDED AND SLICED

1 TABLESPOON FISH SAUCE

2 TEASPOONS OYSTER SAUCE

¼ CUP/60ML/2FL OZ WATER

2 TEASPOONS BROWN SUGAR

250G/8OZ (½LB) BROCCOLI, BROKEN INTO FLORETS

20 FRESH BASIL LEAVES

1. Heat oil in wok or frying pan, add garlic and fry for 30 seconds. Add chicken and chilli and fry until chicken is golden brown.
2. Stir in fish sauce, oyster sauce, water, brown sugar and broccoli and stir-fry for 2 minutes.
3. Add basil and toss through. Serve with steamed long-grain rice.
SERVES 4

CHICKEN WITH SHALLOTS AND GINGER

4 DRIED CHINESE MUSHROOMS

1 TABLESPOON OIL

2 CLOVES GARLIC, CHOPPED

500G/1LB CHICKEN THIGH FILLETS, CUT INTO SMALL CUBES

1 TABLESPOON FISH SAUCE

1 TABLESPOON OYSTER SAUCE

¼ CUP/60ML/2FL OZ WATER

1 TABLESPOON LEMON JUICE

2.5CM/1IN CUBE PEELED FRESH GINGER, CUT INTO THIN STRIPS

6 SPRING ONIONS, CUT INTO 2.5CM/1IN LENGTHS

1. Soak mushrooms in hot water for 30 minutes. Drain well and slice thinly.
2. Heat oil in a wok or large frying pan. Add garlic and chicken and fry until chicken is golden brown and cooked through.
3. Stir in all remaining ingredients and stir-fry for 1 minute. Serve with steamed long-grain rice.
SERVES 4

Opposite: Chicken with Shallots and Ginger

Chicken with Basil and Broccoli

Vegetables

PUMPKIN WITH CHILLI AND GARLIC

500G/1LB PUMPKIN

3 TABLESPOONS OIL

1 ONION, CHOPPED

2 CLOVES GARLIC, CRUSHED

3 EGGS

1 GREEN CHILLI, SEEDED AND CHOPPED

2 TEASPOONS FISH SAUCE

1. Peel pumpkin, cut into small chunks and slice thinly. Heat oil in a large frying pan. Add pumpkin, onion and garlic and fry over a moderate heat until pumpkin is soft, turning occasionally.
2. Beat eggs, chilli and fish sauce together and pour over pumpkin. Cover with a lid and cook until egg is set. Cut into wedges and serve from pan.
SERVES 8

MIXED VEGETABLES IN OYSTER SAUCE

6 STALKS BOK CHOY

2 LARGE CARROTS

200G/7OZ GREEN BEANS

1 TABLESPOON OIL

3 CLOVES GARLIC, CHOPPED

125G/4OZ BEAN SPROUTS

2 TABLESPOONS OYSTER SAUCE

1 TABLESPOON WATER

1 TEASPOON BROWN SUGAR

1. Wash bok choy well and cut into 5cm/2in lengths including green tops. Peel carrots and slice. Top and tail beans and cut into 5cm/2in lengths.
2. Heat oil in a wok or large saucepan. Add garlic and fry for 30 seconds. Add bok choy, carrots and beans and stir-fry for 3 minutes.
3. Add bean sprouts, oyster sauce, water and brown sugar and cook for a further 1 minute. Serve hot with steamed long-grain rice.
SERVES 6

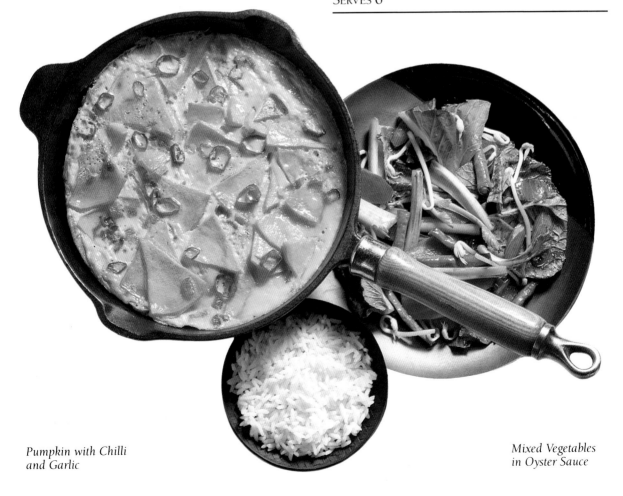

Pumpkin with Chilli and Garlic

Mixed Vegetables in Oyster Sauce

Fried Tofu with Sweet Chilli Sauce

(Bean curd (tofu) is available at health-food shops or Asian food shops. Some are firmer in texture than others so look for one that is firm and easy to cut. Bean curd is made from soy beans and is very high in protein.)

375G/12OZ FIRM BEAN CURD

PLAIN FLOUR

OIL FOR DEEP-FRYING

2 TABLESPOONS CHOPPED PEANUTS

Chilli Sauce

1 TABLESPOON OIL

2 CARROTS, CUT INTO THIN STRIPS

3 CLOVES GARLIC, CHOPPED

3 TABLESPOONS THAI SWEET CHILLI SAUCE

3 TABLESPOONS WATER

1 TABLESPOON FISH SAUCE

4 SPRING ONIONS, SLICED

1. Cut bean curd into 2cm/¾in cubes. Coat lightly in flour, shaking off any excess. Deep-fry in batches until golden brown and crisp, drain on absorbent paper and keep warm in a low oven.
2. *Chilli Sauce:* Heat oil in a saucepan, add carrots and garlic and fry for 2 minutes. Stir in all other sauce ingredients except peanuts and bring to the boil. Lower heat and simmer for 2 minutes or until carrots are tender but still crunchy.
3. Serve sauce over crisp bean curd and sprinkle with chopped peanuts.
Note: Thai Sweet Chilli Sauce is available at Asian food shops and some supermarkets, or use recipe on page 8.
SERVES 4

Fried Tofu with Sweet Chilli Sauce

Crispy Vegetables with Tamarind Dip

VARIETY OF FRESH VEGETABLES, E.G. CAPSICUM (PEPPERS), CARROTS, BEANS, BROCCOLI, CELERY, ZUCCHINI (COURGETTE), CAULIFLOWER

2 EGGS, LIGHTLY BEATEN

PLAIN FLOUR TO COAT

OIL FOR DEEP-FRYING

Tamarind Dip

4 CLOVES GARLIC

2 CORIANDER PLANTS, ROUGHLY CHOPPED

2 TABLESPOONS BROWN SUGAR, WELL PACKED

½ CUP/90G/3OZ PEANUTS

4 TABLESPOONS TAMARIND SAUCE

4 TABLESPOONS WATER

1. Cut vegetables into 7cm/3in lengths or cut into florets. Dip vegetables into egg, then coat in flour, shaking off any excess.
2. Heat oil in a saucepan and deep-fry vegetable pieces a few at a time until golden and crisp. Drain on absorbent paper and keep warm in a low oven while frying the remaining vegetables.
3. *Tamarind Dip:* Place all ingredients in a food processor or blender and process until almost smooth. Spoon into a small bowl and serve with crispy vegetables.
MAKES 1 CUP/250ML/8FL OZ

Opposite: Crispy Vegetables with Tamarind Dip

GREEN CURRY OF VEGETABLES

1 TABLESPOON OIL

1 TABLESPOON GREEN CURRY PASTE (SEE PAGE 72)

1 CUP/250ML/8FL OZ COCONUT MILK

1 LARGE ONION, FINELY CHOPPED

3 DRIED KAFFIR LEAVES

5CM/2IN STRIP LEMON PEEL

2 TABLESPOONS FISH SAUCE

1 MEDIUM EGGPLANT (AUBERGINE)

2 CARROTS

6 SPINACH LEAVES, SHREDDED

2 CUPS/125G/4OZ SHREDDED CHINESE CABBAGE

1. Heat oil in a large saucepan, add curry paste and fry for 1 minute.
2. Stir in coconut milk, onion, kaffir leaves, lemon peel and fish sauce and bring to the boil. Lower heat and simmer for 2 minutes.
3. Cut eggplant into bite-sized chunks and slice carrots, add to pan, cover with a lid and simmer for 5 minutes, or until eggplant is slightly softened.
4. Stir in spinach and cabbage and simmer, covered, for a further 2 to 3 minutes or until spinach is just wilted. Remove kaffir leaves and lemon peel before serving. Serve with steamed long-grain rice.
SERVES 4

STIR-FRIED BROCCOLI AND SHALLOTS

250G/8OZ (½LB) BROCCOLI

1 TABLESPOON OIL

4 SHALLOTS, SLICED

1 CORIANDER PLANT, CHOPPED

1 TABLESPOON FISH SAUCE

1 TABLESPOON WATER

1 TEASPOON BROWN SUGAR

1. Wash broccoli and cut into florets, slice the stalk thinly.
2. Heat oil in a wok or saucepan. Add broccoli and fry for 1 minute. Add all remaining ingredients and stir-fry for 3 minutes or until broccoli is cooked but still crunchy.
SERVES 4

PICKLED VEGETABLES

(White radishes are shaped like a carrot and are white in colour. They are usually quite long and can be up to 35cm/14in in length. If you are unable to purchase them use small red radishes instead. You will need about 25 small red radishes for this recipe.)

1 LONG WHITE RADISH

2 CARROTS

½ CUCUMBER

1 WHITE ONION

3 CUPS/750ML/1¼ PINTS WHITE VINEGAR

1 CUP/250G/8OZ SUGAR

1 TEASPOON SALT

2 RED CHILLIES, SLICED

4 CLOVES GARLIC, CHOPPED

1. Peel radish and carrots and cut into thin strips, about 5cm/2in long and 5mm/¼in wide. Peel cucumber, halve lengthwise, remove seeds and slice. Slice onion thinly.
2. Place vinegar and sugar into a large saucepan and cook, stirring, over a low heat until sugar has dissolved. Bring to boil, add salt, chillies and garlic and boil for 1 minute.
3. Stir in vegetables and bring to the boil. Boil for 1 minute. Pour into a heatproof serving dish or into hot sterilised jars.
4. Allow to cool then refrigerate until ready to serve. They will keep in sterilised jars in the refrigerator for about 2 weeks or in a serving dish for about 1 week. Serve as a salad or as an accompaniment with drinks.
SERVES 6 TO 8

Opposite: Stir-Fried Broccoli and Shallots

Pickled Vegetables

Salads

Green Pawpaw Salad

1 SMALL GREEN PAWPAW, WEIGHT ABOUT 400G/13OZ

2 CARROTS

2 FIRM TOMATOES, CHOPPED

LETTUCE LEAVES OR OTHER SALAD GREENS, E.G. SPINACH, ENDIVE, CABBAGE

2 TABLESPOONS DRIED SHRIMPS, ROUGHLY CHOPPED

Dressing

3 CLOVES GARLIC, CHOPPED

⅓ CUP/80ML/2½FL OZ LEMON JUICE

2 TABLESPOONS FISH SAUCE

1 TABLESPOON BROWN SUGAR

1 RED OR GREEN CHILLI, SEEDED AND CHOPPED

⅓ CUP/60G/2OZ CHOPPED PEANUTS

1. Peel pawpaw and remove seeds. Grate pawpaw and carrot using a food processor (this will give you long thin shreds). Place in a bowl with chopped tomato.
2. *Dressing:* Mix together garlic, lemon juice, fish sauce, brown sugar and chilli. Add to pawpaw mixture with half the peanuts and mix well.
3. Place lettuce or salad greens onto a platter. Spoon pawpaw mixture over greens and sprinkle with remaining peanuts and dried shrimps.
SERVES 6 TO 8

Cucumber Salad

2 MEDIUM GREEN CUCUMBERS

½ WHITE OR RED ONION

Dressing

2 TABLESPOONS WHITE VINEGAR

2 TABLESPOONS LEMON JUICE

1 TABLESPOON FISH SAUCE

2 TABLESPOONS CHOPPED FRESH MINT

2 TEASPOONS WHITE SUGAR

PEPPER TO TASTE

1. Peel cucumbers, halve lengthwise and remove seeds. Grate into long thin shreds or slice very thinly. Slice onion thinly and mix with cucumber in a bowl.
2. *Dressing:* Place all dressing ingredients in a jar and shake well. Pour over cucumber and onion and mix well.
3. Spoon cucumber mixture onto a bed of lettuce to serve. Garnish with cherry tomatoes or red chillies.
SERVES 6

Green Pawpaw Salad

Broccoli and Bean Sprout Salad

500G/1LB BROCCOLI

125G/4OZ BEAN SPROUTS

1 TABLESPOON TOASTED SESAME SEEDS

GINGER DRESSING

2 TEASPOONS FINELY GRATED FRESH GINGER

¼ CUP/60ML/2FL OZ LEMON JUICE

2 TABLESPOONS OIL

3 TEASPOONS CASTER SUGAR

1 TEASPOON FISH SAUCE

1 RED CHILLI, SEEDED AND FINELY CHOPPED

1. Break broccoli into florets and slice stalk thinly. Steam or cook for 2 minutes or until bright green. Be careful not to overcook broccoli, it should still be very crisp. Drain and refrigerate until well chilled.
2. *Ginger Dressing:* Place all dressing ingredients in a jar and shake well.
3. Add bean sprouts to broccoli and place in a salad bowl. Pour over dressing and mix well. Sprinkle with sesame seeds and serve.
SERVES 6

Thai Rice Salad

3 TABLESPOONS OIL

1 TABLESPOON MUSLIM CURRY PASTE (SEE PAGE 72)

1 TABLESPOON BROWN SUGAR

2 TABLESPOONS LEMON JUICE

4 CUPS/750G/1½LB COOKED LONG-GRAIN RICE

1 RED CAPSICUM (PEPPER), CHOPPED

6 SPRING ONIONS, SLICED

440G/14OZ CAN PINEAPPLE PIECES, WELL DRAINED

¼ CUP/10G/⅓OZ CHOPPED MINT

1 CORIANDER PLANT, CHOPPED

SALT TO TASTE

1. Heat 1 tablespoon of the oil in a small frying pan, add curry paste and fry for 1 minute. Remove from heat, add remaining oil, brown sugar and lemon juice.
2. Place rice in a large bowl, add curry mixture and all remaining ingredients and mix well. Refrigerate until ready to serve.
SERVES 6

Opposite: Thai Rice Salad

Broccoli and Bean Sprout Salad

RED AND GREEN SALAD WITH PEANUT DRESSING

3 STICKS CELERY

1 RED CAPSICUM (PEPPER)

6 SPRING ONIONS

200G/7OZ SNOW PEAS (MANGETOUT)

14 CHERRY TOMATOES

ASSORTED SALAD GREENS, E.G. SPINACH, CHICORY, ROCKET, LETTUCE, RADICCHIO

PEANUT DRESSING

⅔ CUP/160ML/5FL OZ LEMON JUICE

1½ TABLESPOONS WHITE SUGAR

1 TABLESPOON FISH SAUCE

1 CORIANDER PLANT, CHOPPED

1 CLOVE GARLIC, CRUSHED

½ CUP/90G/3OZ FINELY CHOPPED PEANUTS

1. Cut all salad vegetables into small pieces that can be easily eaten. Place a layer of salad greens on a large platter and arrange the cut-up vegetables over greens.
2. *Peanut Dressing:* Place all dressing ingredients in a jar and shake well. Pour over salad.
Note: If making the dressing ahead of time, add peanuts just before serving as they will become soggy in the dressing.
SERVES 6 TO 8

TANGY CHICKEN SALAD

1 TABLESPOON OIL

1 SMALL ONION, CHOPPED

500G/1LB CHICKEN FILLET, FINELY CHOPPED

3 TABLESPOONS SNIPPED CHIVES

2 TABLESPOONS CHOPPED MINT

1 GREEN CAPSICUM (PEPPER), CUT INTO VERY THIN STRIPS

6 TO 8 LETTUCE LEAVES, SHREDDED

DRESSING

2 TABLESPOONS LEMON JUICE

1 TABLESPOON FISH SAUCE

1 TABLESPOON BROWN SUGAR, FIRMLY PACKED

FRESHLY GROUND BLACK PEPPER TO TASTE

1. Heat oil in a frying pan. Add onion and chicken and fry until cooked, about 6 to 7 minutes.
2. Remove pan from heat and allow to cool for 5 minutes. Add chives, mint and capsicum, mix well.
3. *Dressing:* Place all dressing ingredients together in a jar and shake well. Add to pan, stirring until well combined.
4. Arrange shredded lettuce on a serving plate and spoon over chicken salad.
SERVES 4

Tangy Chicken Salad

Opposite: Red and Green Salad with Peanut Dressing

Noodles and Curry Pastes

THAI NOODLES

(Traditionally, soft fresh rice noodles are used in this recipe, however they are sometimes difficult to locate so we have substituted Chinese egg noodles which are just as tasty and easier to find.)

200G/7OZ CHINESE EGG NOODLES

2 TABLESPOONS OIL

2 CLOVES GARLIC, CHOPPED

1 ONION, SLICED

200G/7OZ LEAN PORK, CHOPPED

100G/3½OZ PEELED RAW PRAWNS, CHOPPED

¼ CUP/30G/1OZ PICKLED VEGETABLES, CHOPPED, OPTIONAL (SEE PAGE 60)

125G/4OZ FIRM BEAN CURD, CUBED

150G/5OZ BEAN SPROUTS

2 TABLESPOONS FISH SAUCE

2 TABLESPOONS LEMON JUICE

1 TABLESPOON BROWN SUGAR

2 EGGS, LIGHTLY BEATEN

¼ CUP/45G/1½OZ CHOPPED PEANUTS

1 CORIANDER PLANT, CHOPPED

1. Cook the egg noodles in a large saucepan of boiling water until tender, about 5 minutes. Drain well.
2. Heat oil in a wok or frying pan, add garlic, onion and pork and fry until pork is golden.
3. Stir in prawns, pickled vegetables, bean curd, sprouts, fish sauce, lemon juice and brown sugar and cook for 1 minute.
4. Add cooked noodles and push food in pan to one side. Pour in beaten eggs and once they begin to set, mix them lightly through noodles. Add peanuts and cook for 1 minute or until noodles are heated through. Serve sprinkled with chopped coriander.
SERVES 6

CRISPY FRIED NOODLES

(Rice vermicelli is available at most supermarkets or Asian food shops. It is sold in clear cellophane packets in bundles and needs to be broken up before frying. The noodles are white in colour and very thin, and are ideal fried or soaked in warm water then added to a sauce.)

200G/7OZ RICE VERMICELLI

2 CUPS/500ML/16FL OZ VEGETABLE OIL FOR DEEP-FRYING

2 CLOVES GARLIC, CHOPPED

1 ONION, CHOPPED

200G/7OZ CHICKEN FILLETS OR LEAN PORK, FINELY CHOPPED

125G/4OZ PEELED RAW PRAWNS, CHOPPED

2 TABLESPOONS TOMATO SAUCE

2 TABLESPOONS FISH SAUCE

2 TABLESPOONS LEMON JUICE

2 TABLESPOONS BROWN SUGAR

½ BUNCH CHIVES, CUT INTO 2.5CM/1IN LENGTHS

1 RED CHILLI, SLICED

1. Place noodles into a large plastic bag and break into short lengths (the plastic bag will prevent the noodles spilling all over the place).
2. Heat oil in a wok or large saucepan. Add noodles a handful at a time and fry until they puff up and are crisp, this will only take about 1 minute. Drain on absorbent paper.
3. Drain oil from pan leaving about 2 table-spoons. Add garlic, onion and chicken and fry until chicken is golden brown.
4. Stir in prawns, sauces, lemon juice and brown sugar and cook for 1 minute or until prawns are cooked. Add noodles and toss quickly. Serve immediately topped with chives and chilli.
Note: If left to stand the noodles will become soggy, so serve as quickly as possible.
SERVES 4

NOODLES WITH VEGETABLES AND OYSTER SAUCE

200G/7OZ CHINESE EGG NOODLES
4 CHINESE DRIED MUSHROOMS
1 TABLESPOON OIL
3 CLOVES GARLIC, CHOPPED
6 SHALLOTS, SLICED
2 STICKS CELERY, SLICED
1 CAPSICUM (PEPPER), SLICED
2 CUPS/125G/4OZ SHREDDED CABBAGE
3 TABLESPOONS OYSTER SAUCE
1 TABLESPOON FISH SAUCE
1 TABLESPOON BROWN SUGAR
2 TABLESPOONS WATER
¼ CUP/45G/1½OZ CHOPPED PEANUTS

1. Cook egg noodles in a large saucepan of boiling water until tender, about 5 minutes. Drain well. Soak mushrooms in hot water for 20 minutes, then slice thinly.
2. Heat oil in a wok or large frying pan, add garlic and fry for 1 minute.
3. Add all other ingredients except peanuts and noodles, bring to the boil. Lower heat and simmer for 2 minutes or until vegetables are tender but still crunchy.
4. Stir in cooked noodles and heat for 1 minute or until noodles are heated through. Serve sprinkled with peanuts.
SERVES 6

NOODLES IN CHICKEN AND COCONUT SAUCE

200G/7OZ RICE VERMICELLI
1½ CUPS/375ML/12FL OZ COCONUT MILK
2 CLOVES GARLIC, CHOPPED
1 ONION, CHOPPED
200G/7OZ CHICKEN FILLETS, CHOPPED
2 TABLESPOONS FISH SAUCE
2 TEASPOONS TAMARIND SAUCE
2 TEASPOONS BROWN SUGAR
125G/4OZ BEAN SPROUTS
6 SPRING ONIONS, SLICED
LEMON WEDGES
1 RED CHILLI, CHOPPED

1. Soak vermicelli noodles in a bowl of hot water for 15 minutes, drain well.
2. In a large saucepan, bring coconut milk to the boil. Add garlic, onion and chicken, lower heat and simmer for 5 minutes or until chicken is cooked.
3. Stir in fish sauce, tamarind sauce and brown sugar and bring to the boil.
4. Add noodles, sprouts and spring onions and simmer gently for 1 to 2 minutes or until there is only a small amount of liquid in the pan. Serve the noodles with lemon wedges and chopped chilli.
SERVES 4

Noodles in Chicken and Coconut Sauce

Opposite: Noodles with Vegetables and Oyster Sauce

Curry Pastes

Curry pastes form the base of most Thai curries. With the addition of meat or vegetables and coconut milk, plus a few extras such as kaffir leaves and herbs, you will have a delicious, fragrant curry in no time at all.

The following curry pastes can be made ahead and stored in a covered jar in the refrigerator for up to one month or freeze in ice-cube trays and simply pop out the desired amount of paste as needed. This frozen paste will keep in the freezer for 3 months.

Muslim Curry Paste

6 RED CHILLIES

6 CLOVES GARLIC, PEELED

2 ONIONS, QUARTERED

2CM/¾IN CUBE PEELED FRESH GINGER, ROUGHLY CHOPPED

2 STALKS LEMON GRASS, SLICED, OR RIND OF ½ LEMON

1 TABLESPOON GROUND CORIANDER

1 TABLESPOON GROUND CUMIN

1 TEASPOON GROUND CINNAMON

¼ TEASPOON GROUND CLOVES

¼ TEASPOON GROUND CARDAMOM

¼ TEASPOON GROUND BLACK PEPPER

1 TEASPOON SHRIMP PASTE (OPTIONAL)

1. Remove stems from chillies and discard. Place chillies in a food processor or blender with garlic, onions, ginger and lemon grass.
2. Place all remaining spices and shrimp paste into a small frying pan and stir over a low heat for 2 to 3 minutes or until spices begin to give a roasted smell. Remove from heat, cool slightly and add to food processor with other ingredients.
3. Process until mixture is smooth, scraping down sides of bowl in between processing. Store as suggested.
MAKES 1 CUP/250ML/8FL OZ

Green Curry Paste

10 MEDIUM GREEN CHILLIES

6 CLOVES GARLIC, PEELED

1 ONION, QUARTERED

2 CORIANDER PLANTS, ROUGHLY CHOPPED

2CM/¾IN CUBE PEELED FRESH GINGER, ROUGHLY CHOPPED

PEEL OF 1 LIME OR ½ LEMON

1 TEASPOON SHRIMP PASTE (OPTIONAL)

1 TABLESPOON GROUND CORIANDER

2 TEASPOONS GROUND CUMIN

1 TEASPOON SALT

½ TEASPOON GROUND WHITE PEPPER

1. Remove stems from chillies and discard. Place chillies and all other ingredients in a food processor or blender and process until smooth. Store as suggested.
MAKES 1 CUP/250ML/8FL OZ

Red Curry Paste

10 RED CHILLIES

1 LARGE ONION, CHOPPED

4 CLOVES GARLIC, PEELED

2CM/¾IN CUBE PEELED FRESH GINGER, CHOPPED

2 STALKS LEMON GRASS, SLICED OR PEEL OF ½ LEMON

6 CORIANDER ROOTS

1 TABLESPOON GROUND CORIANDER

2 TEASPOONS GROUND CUMIN

2 TEASPOONS SHRIMP PASTE (OPTIONAL)

½ TEASPOON GROUND WHITE PEPPER

½ TEASPOON SALT

1. Remove stems from chillies and discard. Place chillies in a food processor or blender with all other ingredients. Process until smooth. Store as suggested.
MAKES ¾ CUP/180ML/6FL OZ

Opposite: Muslim Curry Paste
Green Curry Paste
Red Curry Paste

Desserts

FRESH FRUIT IN LIME SYRUP

FRESH SEASONAL FRUITS, E.G. PAWPAW, PINEAPPLE,
MANGOES, HONEYDEW MELON, WATERMELON,
PEACHES, ORANGES.

LIME SYRUP

1 CUP/250ML/8FL OZ WATER

1½ CUPS/375G/12OZ SUGAR

2 TABLESPOONS LIME JUICE CORDIAL

2 TEASPOONS LEMON JUICE

---

1. Remove seeds from fruit and peel if necessary. Cut into bite-sized pieces and place into a serving bowl.
2. *Lime Syrup:* Place water and sugar in a small saucepan. Stir over a low heat until sugar has dissolved. Bring to the boil and boil for 15 to 20 minutes or until slightly syrupy. Remove from heat and cool to room temperature.
3. Stir in lime juice cordial and lemon juice and pour over fruits. Refrigerate until well chilled.
Note: Don't pour syrup over fruit too early as fruit will go soft; 1 to 2 hours beforehand is fine.
This amount of Lime Syrup is enough to toss through fruit to serve 8 people. It can be made up to 2 weeks ahead and stored in a jar in the fridge.
SERVES 8

CREAMY SAGO WITH COCONUT MILK

(Sago is available in packets in supermarkets or health-food shops. It is made from the starch of the sago palm and resembles tiny, hard white pearls before cooking. Once cooked it becomes soft and clear and is quite delicious.)

½ CUP/90G/3OZ SAGO

1½ CUPS/375ML/12FL OZ WATER

3 CUPS/750ML/1¼ PINTS COCONUT MILK

2 TABLESPOONS WHITE SUGAR

2 TABLESPOONS BROWN SUGAR, WELL PACKED

¼ TEASPOON SALT

3CM/1¼IN STRIP LEMON PEEL

---

1. Place sago, water and coconut milk in a saucepan and bring to the boil.
2. Add sugars, salt and lemon peel, lower heat and simmer gently for about 25 minutes or until sago is clear and custard has thickened. Remove lemon peel and serve.
SERVES 4

*Fresh Fruit
in Lime Syrup*

MANGOES WITH CREAMY RICE

4 CUPS/1 LITRE/1¾ PINTS COCONUT MILK
½ CUP/110G/3½OZ LONG-GRAIN RICE
¼ CUP/45G/1½OZ BROWN SUGAR
PINCH GROUND CARDAMOM
PINCH SALT
2 TO 3 FRESH MANGOES

1. Place coconut milk, rice, brown sugar, cardamom and salt into an ovenproof dish and mix well.
2. Bake in a moderately slow oven (160°C/325°F) for 1 hour or until rice is cooked and mixture is creamy. Stir occasionally while cooking to break up rice.
3. Peel mangoes and slice flesh. Arrange sliced mango on plates and serve with a large spoonful of the creamy rice.
SERVES 4 TO 6

BANANA AND COCONUT CUSTARD

2 CUPS/500ML/16FL OZ COCONUT MILK
2 TABLESPOONS WHITE SUGAR
¼ TEASPOON SALT
2 TABLESPOONS CORNFLOUR
EXTRA ⅓ CUP/80ML/2½FL OZ COCONUT MILK
3 BANANAS, PEELED AND THICKLY SLICED

1. Place coconut milk, sugar and salt in a saucepan and bring to the boil.
2. Mix cornflour and extra coconut milk together until smooth, add to pan, stirring until custard boils and thickens.
3. Add bananas, lower heat and simmer for 2 minutes or until bananas are tender. Serve hot.
SERVES 4

COCONUT ICE-CREAM

2 CUPS/500ML/16FL OZ COCONUT MILK
½ CUP/125G/4OZ WHITE SUGAR
¼ TEASPOON SALT
1 TEASPOON GELATINE POWDER
1 CUP/250ML/8FL OZ CREAM
1 EGG WHITE, LIGHTLY BEATEN

1. Place coconut milk, sugar and salt in a saucepan. Sprinkle gelatine powder over the top and stir. Bring slowly to the boil, stirring until sugar and gelatine have dissolved. Once mixture has reached the boil remove from heat immediately and cool.
2. Stir in cream and lightly beaten egg white and pour into a cake tin. Freeze until almost set. Place chunks of ice-cream into a food processor and process until smooth. Pour into a plastic freezer container and freeze until ready to serve.
SERVES 6

SUGAR BAKED BANANAS ✓ Don't overcook!

4 BANANAS
2 TABLESPOONS LEMON JUICE
½ CUP/90G/3OZ BROWN SUGAR, LIGHTLY PACKED
2 TABLESPOONS SHREDDED COCONUT

1. Peel bananas and halve lengthwise. Arrange in the base of a shallow ovenproof dish cut-side down.
2. Pour over lemon juice and sprinkle with brown sugar and shredded coconut.
3. Bake in a moderate oven (180°C/350°F) for 10 to 15 minutes or until bananas are tender. Serve with ice-cream.
SERVES 4

Opposite: Sugar Baked Bananas and Coconut Ice-Cream

INGREDIENTS

Basil: Thai basil is similar to our own sweet basil, although it has a slight aniseed flavour and is red coloured around the stem area. Sweet basil has been used in the recipes in this book.

Bean sprouts: Are the sprouts grown from mung beans. They are available in fruit and vegetable shops or in cans in some supermarkets and Asian food shops. They are cream in colour and crunchy in texture.

Bok choy: Is also known as Chinese chard – it has crisp white stems which are similar to silverbeet and green leafy tops. The tops and stems are used in cooking and have a mild flavour and crunchy texture; if unavailable, use young silverbeet or Swiss chard.

Cardamom: Is actually a pod and the cardamom seeds come from within the pod. A recipe will usually ask for cardamom pods, cardamom seeds or ground cardamom. All are readily available in most supermarkets or health food shops.

Chilli: Chillies are members of the capsicum family and there are many different types. The small bird's-eye chillies, red or green, are about 3cm/1¼in long and are the hottest. The larger chillies, about 10cm/4in long, are milder, although don't be fooled – they are still very hot. If you don't want too hot a flavour, use the larger chillies and remove seeds before cooking as these are the hottest part of the chilli. Also the longer the chilli is cooked in the food the more heat it will release. Be careful after handling chilli not to touch eyes or sensitive skin as the chilli will burn. If handling a lot of chilli it is a good idea to wear rubber gloves.

Coconut milk: Is a basic ingredient in Thai cookery and is made by mixing the fresh grated coconut flesh with water and squeezing out the liquid. Canned coconut milk is available in some supermarkets and Asian food shops, although it is sometimes confusingly called coconut cream. Dried coconut milk is also available and is an excellent way of always having fresh coconut milk on hand.

To make your own coconut milk, place 1¼ cups/100g/3½oz desiccated coconut and 1¼ cups/300ml/10fl oz water in a saucepan and bring to the boil. Lower heat and simmer for 5 minutes, stirring once or twice. Strain well, squeezing out as much milk as possible. Discard the remaining coconut. This quantity should give you about 1 cup/250ml/8fl oz coconut milk.

Coriander: Sometimes called Chinese Parsley or Cilantro, it is an essential part of Thai cookery and there is really no substitute for it. The whole of the plant is used – leaves, stem, roots and seeds. Although when buying it fresh, the seeds are not part of the plant – these appear in the mature plant which you will see if you grow your own. Simply pop a few coriander seeds (dried and available in most plant nurseries) into the ground in a sunny spot in the garden and watch them grow. Coriander plants tend to go to seed quickly so ideally you need to keep planting seeds for a regular supply. If a recipe calls for one coriander plant, this is quite simply one root section with the green top attached. Usually it is sold in bunches containing about six to eight plants. It does need to be well washed before using.

Cumin: A most unusually flavoured spice which is available in seeds or ground. It adds a wonderful flavour and cannot be substituted.

Fish sauce: A clear, thin, salty sauce made from fermenting salted fish. It is available from Asian food shops or some supermarkets.

Ginger: Fresh ginger is readily available in fruit shops and some supermarkets. It needs to be peeled and any fibre removed, then it is usually chopped, grated or sliced.

Kaffir lime leaves: The leaves from the kaffir lime add a very special lime flavour to the dish they are used in. They are sold dried in packets in Asian food shops and should be removed from the dish before serving. If you cannot find them, use fresh young lime or lemon leaves.

Lemon grass: Grows in a clump and looks like a reed. It is the tender white bulb at the base of the plant that is used in Thai cooking. Wash each stalk well and slice finely, discarding the tough green top section (this top section can be mixed with boiling water to make a lovely lemon-flavoured tea). Lemon grass can be purchased by the stalk at Asian food stores or larger fruit and vegetable shops. You can buy it growing at some nurseries and plant it so you have a constant supply at home. If you cannot purchase any, substitute the peel of ¼ lemon for 1 stalk of lemon grass.

Mushrooms: Dried Chinese mushrooms are used mainly in soups and some stir-fried dishes. They should be soaked in hot water for at least 30 minutes before using, then drained and sliced. They have a unique flavour and are quite unlike fresh mushrooms in flavour. You can purchase them in Asian food shops.

Oyster sauce: Is a thick brown sauce made from oysters. It adds a slightly salty oyster flavour and is available in jars or bottles at most supermarkets or Asian food shops.

Shrimp, dried: Are available in packets in Asian food shops. They are small prawns that have been dried. Store in an airtight container once opened as they have a rather strong smell.

Shrimp paste: A thick paste made from prawns and salt. It has a very strong flavour and smell but imparts a special flavour to Thai food that cannot be duplicated. It is available in small jars or containers in Asian food shops. After opening, it should be well sealed and stored in the refrigerator.

Straw mushrooms: Are quite different in appearance to ordinary mushrooms. They are small and the tops are oval in shape. They are available canned in Asian food shops and some supermarkets. They should be drained and rinsed lightly before using.

Tamarind sauce: Tamarind adds a tangy flavour to Thai food without being too bitter. The sauce is thick and dark brown in colour, and is available in Asian food shops or some supermarkets.

Turmeric (ground): Is available in powder form and is used extensively in some curry powders for its flavour and yellow colour. It can be purchased in packets or jars.

INDEX